Edexcel International GCSE English Language
Specification A
Revise
Paper One Question Four
Model Answers and Practice
from
GCSEEnglish.uk

Edward Mooney

gcseenglish.uk

Copyright © 2024 by Edward Mooney

All rights reserved. This book or any portion thereof may not be reproduced or used in any manner whatsoever without the express written permission of the publisher except for the use of brief quotations in a book review or scholarly journal.

First Printing: 2024

ISBN 979-8875925290

www.gcseenglish.uk

Contents

Introduction	**1**
1: The Danger of a Single Story	**5**
2: A Passage to Africa	**9**
3: The Explorer's Daughter	**13**
4: Explorers or boys messing about?	**17**
5: Between a Rock and a Hard Place	**21**
6: Young and dyslexic?	**25**
7: A Game of Polo with a Headless Goat	**29**
8: Beyond the Sky and the Earth	**33**
9: H is for Hawk	**37**
10: Chinese Cinderella	**41**
Appendix 1: How will my answer be assessed?	**45**
Appendix 2: Acknowledgements	**47**

Introduction

In this book, you will find the guidance you need to help you improve your Paper One Question Four answers for the Pearson Edexcel International GCSE (9-1) in English Language (Specification A) (4EA1) qualification.

The answers are also valid for the Unit One Question Four answers for the modular version of this qualification: Pearson Edexcel International GCSE in English Language (Specification A) (4XEA1) (Modular).

There are practice exam questions, writing checklists and complete full-marks model answers to help show you what a good answer looks like and what the examiners are looking for. All the questions are based on recent, publicly available past papers.

Each question uses evidence from, and offers interpretations of, each of the texts selected by the exam board for study by students preparing for this qualification, as published in Part 1 (Section A Non-fiction texts) of the *Pearson Edexcel International GCSE Anthology*. Students entered for this exam should be provided with a copy of the anthology by their exam centre and will already be familiar with the ten texts. Alternatively, the anthology is available for free via the following weblink: **www.gcseenglish.uk/anthology/**

How to use this book

There are a range of different ways you can use this book. You could:

- read the answers and see what an excellent exam answer looks like.
- read the exam questions and then plan and write your own answers.
- use the checklists (provided after every answer) to see how many of the writing recommendations are met by each answer.
- use the checklists (provided after every answer) to help you plan and write your own answers.
- read the answers again, more slowly, identifying and remembering key interpretations of the anthology texts.
- re-write the answers using different textual evidence and/or a differing set of interpretations.

Of course, these are practice questions and model answers. Your writing in your exam should be your own work. Don't attempt to memorise an answer and copy it out as you risk being penalised, such as having marks taken away or even being disqualified from the entire exam.

About Interpretation of the Anthology Texts

Interpretation of texts can differ from person to person. You may read interpretations here that are new to you, or you may even disagree with some of the interpretations. This is to be expected, and especially so given the wide range of genres, topics and writing styles selected for the *Pearson Edexcel International GCSE Anthology* by the exam board; there is a whole world of possible, plausible interpretations.

To help you navigate this potentially disorientating web of information, I have kept the interpretations in these answers very close to the mainstream interpretations, versions of which you can readily find in textbooks, revision resources and school handouts. I have also made extensive use of the interpretations identified as top band indicative content in exam board mark schemes, exemplars and training material. My reasonable assumption is: if it is in the mark scheme then it should be in the model answer.

If the mainstream interpretations change (which is entirely possible), then I will update the model answers in future editions.

About timing, answer paper, word count

The paper version of the Paper One exam provides three pages (around 70 lines) of writing space for the answer to Question Four. The onscreen version of the exam software, at the time of writing, has no word/character limit for answers – though this may change as this experimental technology is rolled out.

Whether on paper or on screen, time is very limited for this answer. Students should spend 3 to 5 minutes reading, thinking and selecting quotations before then spending between 20 and 22 minutes writing the answer.

The model answers in this collection are written under these constraints. They are detailed and full, ranging with confidence across the entirety of the text extract. Though it would be challenging for many students to write similarly long answers in the time available, it would not be impossible to do so, especially if practised. If you struggle with timing, you may need to cut one or two paragraphs or slim down some of the paragraphs in order to show the examiner that you have ranged perceptively across the whole of the text.

Finally, given the aforementioned time constraints, it is simply not possible for these answers to offer *every* interpretation or select and examine *every* language and structure technique. Therefore, I had to make tough decisions to incorporate some interpretations, some techniques, but leave out others – and you too will have to make similar tough decisions. If one of your favoured interpretations or techniques is missing from these model answers, go ahead and write your own version.

More about me

I am a qualified teacher of English with a degree in English Literature from the University of Cambridge. I have taught and examined GCSE and A Level English courses at outstanding schools since 2006. I now write model answers and provide exam tuition through my website gcseenglish.uk.

Be the first to learn about new collections of model answers and keep up to date with future projects by subscribing to my newsletter or following my social media channels. Visit gcseenglish.uk or search gcseenglishuk and feel free to leave a review.

Best of luck in your exams!

1: The Danger of a Single Story

Remind yourself of the extract from *'The Danger of a Single Story'* (Text Two in the Extracts Booklet).

Q4

How does the writer, Chimamanda Ngozi Adichie, use language and structure **in Text Two** to convey her thoughts and opinions?

You should support your answer with close reference to the extract, including **brief** quotations.

[12 marks]

1: The Answer

In this speech, Adichie presents her views on the power of storytelling and the danger of seeing the world from a single viewpoint. In her short opening sentence, Adichie announces herself as a "storyteller" and goes on to directly address the audience as "you." This establishes Adichie's credentials to speak about the challenges of storytelling and involves the audience as being not just listeners to an informative speech, but to an intriguing and potentially dramatic personal story.

Adichie begins by using her personal experience of reading to outline her central thesis: consuming stories from one culture only is dangerous. She recounts how the characters in the stories she read as a child "played in the snow…ate apples, and…talked a lot about the weather." She follows up by noting that in Nigeria: "we didn't have snow, we ate mangoes, and we never talked about the weather." Juxtaposing these antithetical lists, crafted with parallel sentence structures, conveys the differences between British culture and Nigerian culture, suggesting that Adichie's experience of reading alienates her from her own culture.

Adichie then uses ethos to show how this alienation led her to be ignorant of her fellow Nigerian citizens. She relates the anecdote of her trip to Fide's village, revealing her ignorance of the creativity of the Nigerian and lower classes by being "startled" at the "beautifully patterned basket" made by Fide's brother. This candid admission of ignorance, shows that Adichie knows she is as guilty as anyone else of making false judgements based on a "single story." This increases our trust in Adichie as, rather than merely berating the audience for their ignorance and prejudice, she presents herself as equally part of the problem, thus giving credibility to her message and making the audience more likely to agree with her subsequent recommendations.

Adiche then turns her attention to how others' narrow-minded understanding of culture led to racist interactions when she lived in the USA. Adichie shows that her roommate's ignorance indicates that she only understood a "single story of Africa: a single story of catastrophe." This parallel construction deliberately links the two final words showing how, for many in developed countries, Africa is understood merely as a place of catastrophe. The audience, most of whom will be people very similar to Adichie's roommate, may well feel an uncomfortable pang of guilt here as we are encouraged to realise that we too may base our 'understanding' of an entire complex continent from a charity television advert.

Adichie then continues her personal *mea culpa* by recounting the ignorance she displayed when visiting Mexico. Expecting to see Mexicans "fleecing," "sneaking," and "being arrested," she is ashamed to realise that they are in fact going about their normal everyday lives. The verbs used in the asyndetic list emphasise the offensive stereotypes of Mexican people that Adichie realises she had unthinkingly believed, further showing how damaging single stories can be.

As the speech draws to its close, Adichie brings all the strands together to argue in favour of widening our cultural experience through actively choosing to read and encounter many stories, rather than one. The danger of the single story that can be "used to dispossess and to malign" is juxtaposed with the value of multifarious stories that "empower and humanize." Again, the parallel construction emphasises the antithesis, thus powerfully promoting the benefits of reading multiple stories.

Finally, Adichie looks ahead positively to a multicultural world of tolerance in which peoples of all cultures learn each other's stories and respect each other. Adichie uses a call to action – "reject the single story" – and ends by echoing another famous writer, Alice Walker, saying that, by seeking out many stories, we may "regain a kind of paradise." The allusion to The Fall suggests the possibility of humanity returning to a life of carefree innocence in the Garden of Eden, while evoking Walker is a use of logos that lends credence to Adichie's recommendation, suggesting that Adichie's ideas are shared by other, respected writers.

1: Answer Writing Checklist

As you read, check how many of the recommendations below are followed by the model answer. Then, use the checklist to help you write your own answer.

Remember that these are *recommendations* from an experienced teacher, not *requirements*. Allow them to help and guide you, but don't allow them to restrict you; if you have a different idea and feel confident about it, then give it a go!

- ☐ Choose quotations from across the entire text.
- ☐ Work through the text from top to bottom.
- ☐ Write PEA-style paragraphs.
- ☐ Use wording of question in answer – "The writer presents/shows/engages etc."
- ☐ Refer to the writer by their surname.
- ☐ Use topic sentences to open each PEA-style paragraph.
- ☐ Use short, precise quotations to support interpretations.
- ☐ Embed quotations fully into the flow of the answer.
- ☐ Write a close analysis of language.
- ☐ Write a close analysis of text structure.
- ☐ Write a close analysis of sentence structure.
- ☐ Use relevant subject terminology.
- ☐ Analyse effect on readers: what do we feel? How are we engaged?
- ☐ Analyse effect on readers: what do we learn?
- ☐ Use accurate spelling, punctuation and grammar.
- ☐ Write as many PEA-style paragraphs as you are able in the time available (c20-22 mins).

2: A Passage to Africa

Remind yourself of the extract from *'A Passage to Africa'* (Text Two in the Extracts Booklet).

Q4

In what ways does the writer use language and structure to show his reactions to the people he encounters in Somalia?

You should support your answer with close reference to the extract, including **brief** quotations.

[12 marks]

2: The Answer

In this extract from his memoir, Alagiah presents his shock upon encountering "a thousand...lean, scared and betrayed faces" whilst reporting on the 1992 famine in Somalia. The large number emphasises the widespread nature of the suffering Alagiah witnessed and the dramatic tricolon of negative adjectives moves from the people's pain to the cause of their pain, betrayal, as Alagiah denounces those who have failed the victims of the famine.

Alagiah then, with striking honesty, goes on to reveal the exploitative attitudes he and other journalists have when covering crises, stating that they are "no longer impressed" by appalling images, instead "craving" for more shocking images of horrifying human despair. This shows how he has become desensitised to what he observes, caring more about pleasing his bosses rather than the dying victims of the famine.

Alagiah's brutal, self-denouncing, honesty continues as he writes openly about the disgust he feels during his encounters with the famine victims, noting that this is "taboo" among journalists, who would normally sanitise their language for broadcast. Alagiah describes the "decaying flesh" and "putrid air" breathed by a "rotting" woman. The sense of smell is invoked to force us to imagine ourselves there with Alagiah and to demonstrate the revulsion he feels as he tours the famine-stricken region.

However, Alagiah also shows that he feels pity and admiration for the victims as he describes how the famine victims "aspire" to "dignity" in impossible conditions. The example of the "dying man who keeps his hoe" near to him, suggests that he hopes he will one day be able to till the fields again, and work to provide for his family. Alagiah, however, knows that this aspiration is futile.

Alagiah then focuses on an encounter with a man who smiled at him. Though only a "fleeting meeting," the encounter is one Alagiah will "never forget" and causes him to ask himself: "what was it about that smile?" The rhyme and the subsequent rhetorical question convey how intrigued Alagiah is by this incongruous gesture, a smile in such suffering, and prefigures the life-changing resolution that Alagiah is about to make.

Alagiah then shows how the man's smile triggers a difficult debate about the role of a journalist in times of human suffering and the relationship "between me and him, between us and him, between the rich world and the poor world." The tricolon zooms out from Alagiah and the man, to journalists in general and then to the people of the developed world who are, of course, Alagiah's readers. We are drawn in to Alagiah's internal debate and challenged to consider our role in the creation of the suffering of those in poorer countries.

Alagiah then shows that his encounter with the famine victims has encouraged him to adopt a more humble attitude. In his final sentence, Alagiah directly addresses the smiling man, calling him his "nameless friend," the noun expressing a degree of closeness; moreover, in his final clause, "I owe you one," he adopts a colloquial phrasing to express his gratitude and to show recognition for the influence that the man unwittingly had over him.

2: Answer Writing Checklist

As you read, check how many of the recommendations below are followed by the model answer. Then, use the checklist to help you write your own answer.

Remember that these are *recommendations* from an experienced teacher, not *requirements*. Allow them to help and guide you, but don't allow them to restrict you; if you have a different idea and feel confident about it, then give it a go!

- ☐ Choose quotations from across the entire text.
- ☐ Work through the text from top to bottom.
- ☐ Write PEA-style paragraphs.
- ☐ Use wording of question in answer – "The writer presents/shows/engages etc."
- ☐ Refer to the writer by their surname.
- ☐ Use topic sentences to open each PEA-style paragraph.
- ☐ Use short, precise quotations to support interpretations.
- ☐ Embed quotations fully into the flow of the answer.
- ☐ Write a close analysis of language.
- ☐ Write a close analysis of text structure.
- ☐ Write a close analysis of sentence structure.
- ☐ Use relevant subject terminology.
- ☐ Analyse effect on readers: what do we feel? How are we engaged?
- ☐ Analyse effect on readers: what do we learn?
- ☐ Use accurate spelling, punctuation and grammar.
- ☐ Write as many PEA-style paragraphs as you are able in the time available (c20-22 mins).

3: The Explorer's Daughter

Remind yourself of the extract from *'The Explorer's Daughter'* (Text Two in the Extracts Booklet).

Q4

How does the writer use language and structure to show her thoughts and feelings about watching the hunt?

You should support your answer with close reference to the extract, including **brief** quotations.

[12 marks]

3: The Answer

In Text Two, Herbert displays the quiet awe and respect she feels while witnessing a narwhal hunt conducted by the indigenous Inughuit of Greenland. She describes gazing over the "glittering kingdom" to see the "spectral play of colour" created by the narwhal spray. The metaphor evokes fairy tales or even Disney films, suggesting that Herbert feels she is witnessing something beautiful, regal and magical.

In fact, Herbert then goes on to wonder if what she is seeing is real. She considers whether the narwhal were merely "mischievous tricks of the shifting light" suggesting that the scene seems unreal, almost ethereal. The language creates a spiritual tone showing how, for Herbert, the hunt is more than simply a blood sport; it is a profoundly important part of a noble culture.

Next, Herbert offers us factual information about the hunt, aiming to justify why the Inughuit engage in this violent activity. She outlines the benefits the Inughuit derive from the dead narwhal's "mattak" and how they use narwhal tusks to create religious artefacts called "tupilaks." The use of the indigenous language here, rather than English, emphasises again that narwhal hunting is a vitally important part of Inughuit culture, providing food, heat, light and spiritual sustenance.

Then, Herbert shows her understanding of the role of the spectating wives in the hunt. A long complex sentence moves from all the women to "each woman focusing on her husband," conveying the intensity of the experience for the observers as they urge the hunters to provide their "staple diet." The adjective here shows, again, that narwhal hunting is not merely a sport but is crucial to their survival.

Herbert's text reaches a climax as she ponders the dilemma the hunt poses her as an outsider with the conservationist attitudes common among Western tourists to the Arctic. She juxtaposes the hunter whom she "urge[s]...on" and the narwhal whom she "urge[s]...to dive, to leave, to survive." The repeated verb emphasises Herbert's mixed feelings yet the tricolon of infinitive verbs directed at the narwhal, complete with powerful rhythm and rhyme, conveys the writer's intense emotional response to the animal and suggests that her sympathies ultimately lie more with the narwhal than the hunters.

However, Herbert shows her understanding of the Inughuit way of life and does not condemn their involvement in hunting. After presenting the beauty and drama of the scene, Herbert focuses on the "harshness" of living in a place where only "one annual supply ship...makes it through the ice." Readers are reminded of the precariousness of Arctic life, and the unspoken comparison with Western life, where supply ships arrive all the time, emphasises once again that hunting is vital for the Inughuit.

Finally, Herbert reaches a powerful conclusion showing her respect for the hardy hunters and their way of life: "hunting is still an absolute necessity in Thule." The final single-clause sentence, with its use of an intensifier, sums up Herbert's thoughts in a strong and unarguable statement, challenging us to rethink our preconceptions about the horror of hunting and, instead, appreciate the importance of hunting for the Inughuit.

3: Answer Writing Checklist

As you read, check how many of the recommendations below are followed by the model answer. Then, use the checklist to help you write your own answer.

Remember that these are *recommendations* from an experienced teacher, not *requirements*. Allow them to help and guide you, but don't allow them to restrict you; if you have a different idea and feel confident about it, then give it a go!

- ☐ Choose quotations from across the entire text.
- ☐ Work through the text from top to bottom.
- ☐ Write PEA-style paragraphs.
- ☐ Use wording of question in answer – "The writer presents/shows/engages etc."
- ☐ Refer to the writer by their surname.
- ☐ Use topic sentences to open each PEA-style paragraph.
- ☐ Use short, precise quotations to support interpretations.
- ☐ Embed quotations fully into the flow of the answer.
- ☐ Write a close analysis of language.
- ☐ Write a close analysis of text structure.
- ☐ Write a close analysis of sentence structure.
- ☐ Use relevant subject terminology.
- ☐ Analyse effect on readers: what do we feel? How are we engaged?
- ☐ Analyse effect on readers: what do we learn?
- ☐ Use accurate spelling, punctuation and grammar.
- ☐ Write as many PEA-style paragraphs as you are able in the time available (c20-22 mins).

4: Explorers or boys messing about?

Remind yourself of the extract from 'Explorers or boys messing about?' (Text Two in the Extracts Booklet).

Q4

How does the writer use language and structure **in Text Two** to show what people thought about the actions of the two explorers?

You should support your answer with close reference to the extract, including **brief** quotations.

[12 marks]

4: The Answer

In his article, Morris immediately expresses his doubts about the explorers. The headline, "boys messing about," is posed as a rhetorical question, thus undermining and infantilising the two men, implying a lack of professionalism. We later find out that it was one of the explorer's wives, Jo Vestey, who used the dismissive phrase, suggesting her lack of respect for her husband's exploits.

Morris offers expert opinion on the explorers' predicament to further show his own sense that they were foolish amateurs. He twice notes that "experts questioned the[ir] wisdom" and, in particular, lists Günter Endres' credentials as "editor of Jane's Helicopter Market and Systems" to demonstrate his expertise, in stark contrast to the dilettante explorers who chose to use a small, single engine helicopter for such a difficult expedition.

Morris then zooms in on an apparently incidental detail to emphasise the explorers' wealth, implying that Morris feels these men had more money than sense. He notes that Steve Brooks was given an expensive "Breitling emergency watch" to suggest that he is indulged and enjoys expensive 'toys'. It also suggests that Brooks' long-suffering wife expected he would get into difficulty, showing again how ill-suited he was for his expedition.

Morris continues to show his disdain for the explorers by setting up a contrast between them and their rescuers. He praises the HMS Endurance's genuine mission of "surveying uncharted waters" and juxtaposes this with his questioning of what the two explorers "were trying to achieve." This favourably contrasts the Royal Navy's endurance with the explorers' frailty and shows just how pointless Morris perceives the explorers' expedition to be.

Morris continues to quote expert opinion to back up his scathing review of their actions. An "Antarctic explorer," who would be an expert in such an environment, claims the explorers' survival to be "nothing short of a miracle" which shows his belief that they were unprepared for the hostile conditions. The religious hyperbole also suggests that the rescuers are almost god-like in their ability, creating, again, a yawning contrast between the capable rescue team and the useless explorers.

Subsequently, Morris draws attention to the explorers' previous exploits in order to show just how immature they are. An attempt to forge relations "between east and west" was stymied by Russian authorities threatening to "scramble military helicopters." Again, a contrast is created, this time presenting the explorers as dangerously naive, willing to risk death or even military escalation for an adventurous helicopter ride. The explorers' small helicopter is also juxtaposed with the forbidding attack helicopters, suggesting that, had the situation spiralled out of control, the explorers would have been killed.

Finally, Morris concludes his demolition of Brooks and Smith by quoting Jo Vestey's dismissal of them. She comments that the two men "will probably have their bottoms kicked and be sent home the long way." These patronising comments portray the men as immature children who deserve punishment and humiliation in order to learn their lesson and stop planning such foolish escapades.

4: Answer Writing Checklist

As you read, check how many of the recommendations below are followed by the model answer. Then, use the checklist to help you write your own answer.

Remember that these are *recommendations* from an experienced teacher, not *requirements*. Allow them to help and guide you, but don't allow them to restrict you; if you have a different idea and feel confident about it, then give it a go!

- [ ] Choose quotations from across the entire text.
- [ ] Work through the text from top to bottom.
- [ ] Write PEA-style paragraphs.
- [ ] Use wording of question in answer – "The writer presents/shows/engages etc."
- [ ] Refer to the writer by their surname.
- [ ] Use topic sentences to open each PEA-style paragraph.
- [ ] Use short, precise quotations to support interpretations.
- [ ] Embed quotations fully into the flow of the answer.
- [ ] Write a close analysis of language.
- [ ] Write a close analysis of text structure.
- [ ] Write a close analysis of sentence structure.
- [ ] Use relevant subject terminology.
- [ ] Analyse effect on readers: what do we feel? How are we engaged?
- [ ] Analyse effect on readers: what do we learn?
- [ ] Use accurate spelling, punctuation and grammar.
- [ ] Write as many PEA-style paragraphs as you are able in the time available (c20-22 mins).

5: Between a Rock and a Hard Place

Remind yourself of the extract from *'Between a Rock and a Hard Place'* (Text Two in the Extracts Booklet).

Q4

How does the writer use language and structure to interest and engage the reader?

You should support your answer with close reference to the extract, including **brief** quotations.

[12 marks]

5: The Answer

In his first-hand account, Ralston presents the danger he faced during a solo wilderness hike. Presented in the present tense that conveys a sense of dramatic immediacy, the text emphasises the cramped "claustrophobic" nature of the canyon. This, plus the "refrigerator chockstone" looming over Ralston, foreshadows future danger, suggesting the possibility of falling rocks crushing whatever, or whoever, is below.

Ralston then explains how he would usually climb in a canyon like this one. He refers to "stemming or chimneying." The jargon suggests that he is an experienced climber, but Ralston injects a note of uncertainty by saying that only "sometimes" are these techniques "possible." The reader realises that Ralston's current situation may not be one of those times, foreshadowing that this hypothetical presentation of best practice may not be what we are about to witness.

Ralston continues to build tension in the early part of the extract, narrating his movement through the canyon onto a large chockstone that "teeters" under his weight. This verb, associated with wobbling on a cliff edge or a 'teeter-totter' (the American name for a see-saw) conveys how precarious Ralston's situation is, suggesting that only the smallest movement could see him tumbling to his doom.

Ralston then describes in cinematic detail the moment that a rock falls and crushes his hand. As he watches the rock fall, "time dilates" and his "reactions decelerate." This creates a sense of slow-motion movement and increases the horror of the scene by suggesting that Ralston may have had time to move out from under the rock but that, transfixed by the "backlit chockstone," he can only watch it fall. The subsequent long complex sentence further suggests that time has slowed down and serves to emphasise Ralston's panic.

Next, Ralston zooms in on how destructive the falling rock is. A series of powerful verbs emphasises the rock's formidable force: "smashes," "yank," "ricochets," "crushes," "ensnares," "tearing." The shift in pace from the previous slow-motion sequence, coupled with the violence of the verbs, reinforces the horror experienced by Ralston, filling readers with a sense of dread as we realise that he is now trapped.

This dread is enhanced as Ralston presents his dramatic reaction to his predicament. Seeking supernatural aid by crying out to "good God" suggests that Ralson fears his death is near as the "flaring agony" and "searing-hot pain," with their connotations of fire, convey the extent of the pain he is experiencing. Readers, aware that Ralston is alone and has not told anyone his hiking plans may well believe, for a moment, that Ralston will die alone, his body never found.

After the drama, movement and noise of the previous paragraphs, Ralston now emphasises the eerie silence of the scene. The final three paragraphs all end with short impactful sentences: "Then silence." "But I'm stuck." "Nothing." These sentences feel more like fragments than complete thoughts, suggesting the shock Ralston may well be experiencing as sensations, ideas, hopes and half-thoughts rush through his consciousness. The three sentences also emphasise Ralston's isolation and the sense that his terrible predicament is impossible to escape from. Knowing he lives to write the text, however, reassures us that he does indeed survive so we now wonder, full of suspense, what remarkable event or effort could possibly lead to Ralston's escape.

5: Answer Writing Checklist

As you read, check how many of the recommendations below are followed by the model answer. Then, use the checklist to help you write your own answer.

Remember that these are *recommendations* from an experienced teacher, not *requirements*. Allow them to help and guide you, but don't allow them to restrict you; if you have a different idea and feel confident about it, then give it a go!

- ☐ Choose quotations from across the entire text.
- ☐ Work through the text from top to bottom.
- ☐ Write PEA-style paragraphs.
- ☐ Use wording of question in answer – "The writer presents/shows/engages etc."
- ☐ Refer to the writer by their surname.
- ☐ Use topic sentences to open each PEA-style paragraph.
- ☐ Use short, precise quotations to support interpretations.
- ☐ Embed quotations fully into the flow of the answer.
- ☐ Write a close analysis of language.
- ☐ Write a close analysis of text structure.
- ☐ Write a close analysis of sentence structure.
- ☐ Use relevant subject terminology.
- ☐ Analyse effect on readers: what do we feel? How are we engaged?
- ☐ Analyse effect on readers: what do we learn?
- ☐ Use accurate spelling, punctuation and grammar.
- ☐ Write as many PEA-style paragraphs as you are able in the time available (c20-22 mins).

6: Young and dyslexic?

Remind yourself of the extract from *'Young and dyslexic?'* (Text Two in the Extracts Booklet).

Q4

How does the writer, Benjamin Zephaniah, use language and structure **in Text Two** to interest and engage the reader?

You should support your answer with close reference to the extract, including **brief** quotations.

[12 marks]

6: The Answer

In this article, Zephaniah aims to reveal to the reader the difficulties he experienced in the education system as a child with dyslexia. He opens with a powerful parallel structure, making use of the first-person plural pronoun: "we are the architects, we are the designers." This reference to respected professions suggests how creative and constructive people with dyslexia can be, whilst connecting the writer with his readers.

Zephaniah then recounts anecdotes about his time in school to demonstrate how misunderstood dyslexia was in the 1960s. The tricolon of negative anaphora – "no compassion, no understanding and no humanity" – emphasises how harshly he was treated at school and Zephaniah's subsequent metaphor – "the past is a different kind of country" – with its echoing of a famous literary quote (L. P. Hartley: "The past is a foreign country: they do things differently there."), highlights how dramatically attitudes to dyslexia have changed since his youth.

Zephaniah further interests the reader by including lines of direct speech. He quotes his teachers' harsh dismissal of his obvious intellectual talents: "Shut up, stupid boy...How dare you challenge me?" This shocking disrespect emphasises the scale of the challenge Zephaniah faced, as he aimed to carve out a career in writing without any help or encouragement from his teachers.

Next, Zephaniah explains how, against considerable odds, he has avoided prison, a fate, he notes, awaits many black men with similar life stories to him. He offers the opinion that staying out of prison is due to "conquering your fears and finding your path in life." The metaphors of conquest and exploration show how he feels that life can sometimes feel like a battle or a journey into the unknown.

Later, Zephaniah gives details about his later career to show how he was able to succeed in spite of his inauspicious start in life: "I wrote more poetry, novels for teenagers, plays, other books and recorded music." The list is long and varied and may provoke a sense of admiration in the reader as we realise the extent of his achievements.

Towards the end of the article, Zephaniah directly addresses young dyslexic readers, encouraging them to feel no shame about dyslexia. He links the prejudice he experienced to racial prejudice saying: "it's not my problem, it's theirs." He then echoes this attitude using the second-person pronoun: "just remember: it's not you." The suggestion is that the problems experienced by many people with dyslexia are not the fault of the individual but of a society that teaches prejudice and ignorance. Zephaniah encourages his readers to be strong and face down that prejudice.

Finally, Zephaniah returns to re-state his main message about the often-overlooked creativity of people with dyslexia, aiming to shift society's focus from the perceived failings of dyslexic people to a consideration the failings of others: "bloody non-dyslexics ... who do they think they are?" The rhetorical question may cause the reader, many of whom will be said 'non-dyslexics,' to ponder the answer and to interrogate how their own prejudices may well have been shaped by the very ignorance attacked by Zephaniah.

6: Answer Writing Checklist

As you read, check how many of the recommendations below are followed by the model answer. Then, use the checklist to help you write your own answer.

Remember that these are *recommendations* from an experienced teacher, not *requirements*. Allow them to help and guide you, but don't allow them to restrict you; if you have a different idea and feel confident about it, then give it a go!

- [ ] Choose quotations from across the entire text.
- [ ] Work through the text from top to bottom.
- [ ] Write PEA-style paragraphs.
- [ ] Use wording of question in answer – "The writer presents/shows/engages etc."
- [ ] Refer to the writer by their surname.
- [ ] Use topic sentences to open each PEA-style paragraph.
- [ ] Use short, precise quotations to support interpretations.
- [ ] Embed quotations fully into the flow of the answer.
- [ ] Write a close analysis of language.
- [ ] Write a close analysis of text structure.
- [ ] Write a close analysis of sentence structure.
- [ ] Use relevant subject terminology.
- [ ] Analyse effect on readers: what do we feel? How are we engaged?
- [ ] Analyse effect on readers: what do we learn?
- [ ] Use accurate spelling, punctuation and grammar.
- [ ] Write as many PEA-style paragraphs as you are able in the time available (c20-22 mins).

7: A Game of Polo with a Headless Goat

Remind yourself of the extract from *'A Game of Polo with a Headless Goat'* (Text Two in the Extracts Booklet).

Q4

How does the writer, Emma Levine, use language and structure **in Text Two** to present Yaqoob and Iqbal?

You should support your answer with close reference to the extract, including **brief** quotations.

[12 marks]

7: The Answer

Initially, in this extract from her travelogue about unusual Asian sports, Levine presents how her travel companions, Yaqoob and Iqbal, react to the possibility of watching a donkey race. The "lads" are "suddenly fired up with enthusiasm." The metaphor suggests a sudden burst of fervour contrasting with their previous lack of interest. The guides' youth is emphasised by referring to them as "lads" and foreshadows the surprising climax to the extract which will reveal that they are not old enough to drive.

Levine then narrates how they join the race. She shows that Yaqoob "edge[s] out" and then "swerves" into the traffic. These contrasting verbs suggest a paradoxical mix of caution and recklessness in Yaqoob's driving and emphasises the noise, chaos and danger of the event, allowing readers to feel immersed in the action.

The danger of the scene, and Yaqoob and Iqbal's excitement, is further emphasised when Levine compares the race to "Formula One without rules." The comparison of donkey racing to the expensive, glamorous and extremely high-speed world of Formula One racing creates a humorous contrast. Readers, imagining the comic sight of donkeys racing at hundreds of miles per hour, sense that, though dangerous, the event is fun.

However, Levine then employs the terminology of evolutionary theory to explain that, for the car drivers, following the race "was survival of the fittest;" the superlative implies that Yaqoob is superior to other drivers and the allusion to Darwin suggests, perhaps hyperbolically, that the race is an event from which only one driver may emerge alive.

Despite this apparent danger, Levine highlights how enjoyable the race is, noting that "Yaqoob loved it." This simple, very short sentence, juxtaposed with the longer, more complex sentences that surround it, emphasises the thrill Yaqoob experiences during the race and suggests that his response is visceral, almost irrational, a physical enjoyment of being so close to disaster.

Levine draws the passage to an unexpected climax by presenting how Yaqoob and Iqbal help her to escape from the dangerous violence that almost spills over as a result of an accident. The tension is undercut by the revelation that Yaqoob does not have a driving licence "because I'm underage!" This, and he and Iqbal's laughter, shows his casual attitude and reveals just how young he must be; the exclamation mark helps to emphasise the writer's shock which is shared by the reader.

Levine ends the extract with a sense of understated anticlimax as she reflects on what could have happened: "a massive pile-up...could have caused problems." This shows just how much danger Levine and her travel companions were in, but also emphasises Yaqoob's happy-go-lucky cavalier attitude. The reader is left with a sense of relief that the worst didn't happen but also a sense of excitement at being able to travel with Levine on her journey and to witness, with her, such an unfamiliar event.

7: Answer Writing Checklist

As you read, check how many of the recommendations below are followed by the model answer. Then, use the checklist to help you write your own answer.

Remember that these are *recommendations* from an experienced teacher, not *requirements*. Allow them to help and guide you, but don't allow them to restrict you; if you have a different idea and feel confident about it, then give it a go!

- [ ] Choose quotations from across the entire text.
- [ ] Work through the text from top to bottom.
- [ ] Write PEA-style paragraphs.
- [ ] Use wording of question in answer – "The writer presents/shows/engages etc."
- [ ] Refer to the writer by their surname.
- [ ] Use topic sentences to open each PEA-style paragraph.
- [ ] Use short, precise quotations to support interpretations.
- [ ] Embed quotations fully into the flow of the answer.
- [ ] Write a close analysis of language.
- [ ] Write a close analysis of text structure.
- [ ] Write a close analysis of sentence structure.
- [ ] Use relevant subject terminology.
- [ ] Analyse effect on readers: what do we feel? How are we engaged?
- [ ] Analyse effect on readers: what do we learn?
- [ ] Use accurate spelling, punctuation and grammar.
- [ ] Write as many PEA-style paragraphs as you are able in the time available (c20-22 mins).

8: Beyond the Sky and the Earth

Remind yourself of the extract from *Beyond the Sky and the Earth* (Text Two in the Extracts Booklet).

Q4

How does the writer, Jamie Zeppa, use language and structure **in Text Two** to interest the reader?

You should support your answer with close reference to the extract, including **brief** quotations.

[12 marks]

8: The Answer

In this extract from her memoir, Zeppa creates a powerful evocation of experiencing a different and unfamiliar culture for the first time. She focuses initially on Bhutan's topography, rejected plate tectonics in favour of the more fanciful analogy of "a giant child" sculpting the landscape, a process Zeppa expresses with a series of powerful, precise verbs with elements of alliteration: "gathering," "piling," "pinching," "knuckling," "poking." This engages us by suggesting that the land is mythical and fantastical, implying that Zeppa, and the reader, are leaving behind the mundane Western world and entering a new, exciting realm.

Zeppa continues to emphasise Bhutan's dramatic landscape by focusing on the mountains. She uses a tricolon, "mountains, more mountains and mountains again," to suggest that the mountains seem endless, expanding as far as the eye can see. In fact, the plural noun "mountains" is repeated eight times in the first two paragraphs, emphasising how many there are and perhaps indicating how impressed or overwhelmed Zeppa is by them. For the reader, likely a low altitude city dweller, the sense that Bhutan is a place beyond our imagining is only heightened.

Zeppa then zooms in the focus on her new life as a teacher, presenting the uncertainty and excitement of her first days in Bhutan. After the wonder of the landscape, Zeppa creates a bathetic, almost comic, fall by describing the disappointing hotel breakfast: "instant coffee, powdered milk, plasticky white bread and flavorless red jam." The list conveys how unappetising the food is and shows that it is a Western-style breakfast, which might surprise readers who may expect a more Bhutanese style of food.

However, as Zeppa goes out into Thimpu for the first time, she shows that Bhutanese architecture is unique and reflects Buddhist culture. Zeppa describes the "lotus flowers, jewels and clouds" painted onto buildings. The tricolon makes the buildings sound exotic and attractive and creates a stark contrast with the repetitive items available for sale in the shops: "Bourbon Biscuits, Coconut Crunchies and the hideously colored Orange Cream Biscuits." The tricolon here emphasises the contrast with the exotic architecture and recalls Zeppa's unappetising breakfast. Readers may be intrigued that the food of the Himalayan nation does not appear to reflect the unique culture of Bhutan.

However, Zeppa then goes on to describe the people and the clothes of Bhutan, focusing on their unique and beautiful nature. She describes the "handsome," "beautiful" people and their clothes: "gho" and "kira." The inclusion of these Bhutanese words, presented in italics, emphasises the exotic culture of Bhutan whilst also showing Zeppa beginning the process of learning the language which, as she translates the words, we are invited to learn alongside her.

This process of learning continues as Zeppa recounts some of the information learnt in her cultural immersion course. She focuses in particular on an amusing account of how a British envoy, Ashley Eden, made a "disastrous visit" to try to prevent the Bhutanese raiding British controlled India and was treated unceremoniously by them. This presents Bhutan as the plucky underdog in the "Great Game" of imperial expansion and confrontation, and Zeppa clearly enjoys recounting Eden's humiliation, encouraging readers to laugh at his arrogance and evoking sympathy for the proud Bhutanese.

Zeppa ends the extract on an upbeat note as she celebrates Bhutan's independence. She writes that she is "full of admiration for this small country." This shows how the Canadian Zeppa, a citizen of the second largest country in the world, itself a creation of British imperialism, is amazed but also happy that this small, remote country, sandwiched between empires, was able to resist being gobbled up and instead thrives as a place with a unique and proud culture. We are left with a very positive impression of Bhutan, and we feel excitement for Zeppa as she continues her journey into the heart of the Himalayas.

8: Answer Writing Checklist

As you read, check how many of the recommendations below are followed by the model answer. Then, use the checklist to help you write your own answer.

Remember that these are *recommendations* from an experienced teacher, not *requirements*. Allow them to help and guide you, but don't allow them to restrict you; if you have a different idea and feel confident about it, then give it a go!

- [ ] Choose quotations from across the entire text.
- [ ] Work through the text from top to bottom.
- [ ] Write PEA-style paragraphs.
- [ ] Use wording of question in answer – "The writer presents/shows/engages etc."
- [ ] Refer to the writer by their surname.
- [ ] Use topic sentences to open each PEA-style paragraph.
- [ ] Use short, precise quotations to support interpretations.
- [ ] Embed quotations fully into the flow of the answer.
- [ ] Write a close analysis of language.
- [ ] Write a close analysis of text structure.
- [ ] Write a close analysis of sentence structure.
- [ ] Use relevant subject terminology.
- [ ] Analyse effect on readers: what do we feel? How are we engaged?
- [ ] Analyse effect on readers: what do we learn?
- [ ] Use accurate spelling, punctuation and grammar.
- [ ] Write as many PEA-style paragraphs as you are able in the time available (c20-22 mins).

9: H is for Hawk

Remind yourself of the extract from '*H is for Hawk*' (Text Two in the Extracts Booklet).

Q4

How does the writer, Helen Macdonald, use language and structure **in Text Two** to build up suspense and tension?

You should support your answer with close reference to the extract, including **brief** quotations.

[12 marks]

9: The Answer

In this extract from her memoir, Macdonald initially creates a sense of tension by gradually revealing what is within the box. She describes how the man "squinted into its dark interior" and then uses onomatopoeia, "thump," to create a sense of mystery and then to suggest that there is something powerful and dangerous within the flimsy box. Readers may fear that the creature could burst out at any moment.

Macdonald then continues to build suspense by slowing the pace of the text and presenting in detail the process of opening the box. A series of short minor sentences – "Concentration. Infinite caution" – impart an impressionistic, slow-motion atmosphere to this moment and convey how delicate the situation is, while the final moment before the bird is revealed is described as "the last few seconds before a battle." The metaphor raises the tension by suggesting that the following scene may be one of conflict.

Suspense then rises dramatically as Macdonald describes the hawk for the first time. A range of powerful metaphors are presented in another series of impressionistic short sentences: "a reptile. A fallen angel…A broken marionette." These suggest that the bird appears ragged, exuding evil and shows Macdonald's disorientated whirl of emotions, simultaneously attracted to, and repulsed by, the hawk. However, the subsequent simile – "like gold falling through water" – suggests the hawk is in fact something beautiful and very precious.

Macdonald then goes on to increase suspense even more by revealing a twist to this tale. A single-line paragraph of four short blunt sentences powerfully conveys the writer's apprehension and dawning realisation that this is not the right bird. This is confirmed by the monosyllabic exclamation of shock and uncertainty, "oh," which, italicised and isolated on the page, momentarily suspends the movement of the narrative, leaving the reader to wonder what might follow.

Subsequently, Macdonald builds suspense by introducing the bigger, and even more threatening, hawk that has been assigned to her. The bird is described as exiting the box "like a Victorian melodrama: a sort of madwoman in the attack." The simile suggests something dark and Gothic, and the play on words ("attack" echoing the more familiar attic) alludes to the nineteenth century novel *Jane Eyre* in which a mysterious woman is imprisoned in an attic but periodically escapes to inflict misery on the people living below. The insinuation is that there is something exaggeratedly menacing and sinister about the bird.

Macdonald then raises the tension more by portraying her conflicted emotions as she contemplates the different, bigger hawk. She presents her thoughts in italics: "This is my hawk." "This isn't my hawk." "But this isn't my hawk." The antithetical statements followed by repetition draw attention to Macdonald's feelings of disbelief and dread, suggesting that, for a moment, she doesn't know what to do.

Finally, the extract finishes on a high moment of suspense as, following Macdonald's "crazy barrage of incoherent appeals...there was a moment of total silence." This presents Macdonald's desperation at this moment, as she pleads with the man but ultimately realises that she may be unsuccessful in her attempt to take the smaller hawk. Readers are left to ponder the outcome and how this will affect Macdonald's difficult journey of recovery from grief at her father's death.

9: Answer Writing Checklist

As you read, check how many of the recommendations below are followed by the model answer. Then, use the checklist to help you write your own answer.

Remember that these are *recommendations* from an experienced teacher, not *requirements*. Allow them to help and guide you, but don't allow them to restrict you; if you have a different idea and feel confident about it, then give it a go!

- [ ] Choose quotations from across the entire text.
- [ ] Work through the text from top to bottom.
- [ ] Write PEA-style paragraphs.
- [ ] Use wording of question in answer – "The writer presents/shows/engages etc."
- [ ] Refer to the writer by their surname.
- [ ] Use topic sentences to open each PEA-style paragraph.
- [ ] Use short, precise quotations to support interpretations.
- [ ] Embed quotations fully into the flow of the answer.
- [ ] Write a close analysis of language.
- [ ] Write a close analysis of text structure.
- [ ] Write a close analysis of sentence structure.
- [ ] Use relevant subject terminology.
- [ ] Analyse effect on readers: what do we feel? How are we engaged?
- [ ] Analyse effect on readers: what do we learn?
- [ ] Use accurate spelling, punctuation and grammar.
- [ ] Write as many PEA-style paragraphs as you are able in the time available (c20-22 mins).

10: Chinese Cinderella

Remind yourself of the extract from *'Chinese Cinderella'* (Text Two in the Extracts Booklet).

Q4

How does the writer use language and structure **in Text Two** to present her relationships with her family and other people?

You should support your answer with close reference to the extract, including **brief** quotations.

[12 marks]

10: The Answer

Initially, in this extract from her autobiography, Mah shows how her younger self is unable to focus whilst playing Monopoly with her school friends because of her worry about leaving school. The worry is described using the simile "throbbed... like a persistent toothache" yet Mah does not confide her fears to her friends. This suggests that she feels distant from them, perhaps unwilling to reveal her fears.

Next, Mah presents how her younger self and her school companions demonstrate respect for their teacher, Ma-mien Valentino, by standing up when she enters. However, the teacher utters three short sentences to Adeline, two of which are peremptory exclamations, ("Hurry up downstairs!") suggesting that she might be irritated that Adeline has not responded more swiftly.

Mah then shows the distant relationship she has with her father by showing that her younger self was "summoned" to discuss her future. She refers to her father's office as "the Holy of Holies." This hyperbolic reference to the office as God's dwelling place, an allusion to Old Testament narratives of Israelite religious practice, suggests that Mah views her father as god-like and feels great fear on entering his presence, requiring permission to do so.

Mah subsequently presents her younger self's conflicting emotions – relief and then trepidation – as she meets her father for the first time in a long time. She poses rhetorical questions to herself: "Is this a giant ruse...? Dare I let my guard down?" The shift into the present tense here emphasises the immediacy and strength of her feelings and shows her lack of trust in her father and her fear that she might be tricked somehow.

However, Mah then shows a dramatic change in tone as she presents her father's happiness at her recent writing competition success. The moment brings Mah "all the joy in the world" and she "only had to stretch out my hand to reach the stars." This hyperbole emphasises the great joy she feels at pleasing her father and also suggests that she is hopeful that it will enable her to achieve her ambition.

Mah then presents more of her conversation with her father where we see more clearly the power differential between them: he, the authoritarian patriarch and she, the timid supplicant. Her father shifts rapidly from laughing "approvingly" to sarcastically "scoff[ing]." The section of direct speech shows how swiftly her father's attitude can change and further reinforces for us the sense that Mah is standing meekly before a capricious god figure, at the mercy of his emotions and whims.

Finally, Mah reveals how, despite not being allowed by her father to choose her own university course, she is happy to be able to continue her education in England. She responds: "thank you very, very much." This repetition shows Mah's gratitude to her father and emphasises the humility she needs to navigate her relationship with her powerful father.

10: Answer Writing Checklist

As you read, check how many of the recommendations below are followed by the model answer. Then, use the checklist to help you write your own answer.

Remember that these are *recommendations* from an experienced teacher, not *requirements*. Allow them to help and guide you, but don't allow them to restrict you; if you have a different idea and feel confident about it, then give it a go!

- ☐ Choose quotations from across the entire text.
- ☐ Work through the text from top to bottom.
- ☐ Write PEA-style paragraphs.
- ☐ Use wording of question in answer – "The writer presents/shows/engages etc."
- ☐ Refer to the writer by their surname.
- ☐ Use topic sentences to open each PEA-style paragraph.
- ☐ Use short, precise quotations to support interpretations.
- ☐ Embed quotations fully into the flow of the answer.
- ☐ Write a close analysis of language.
- ☐ Write a close analysis of text structure.
- ☐ Write a close analysis of sentence structure.
- ☐ Use relevant subject terminology.
- ☐ Analyse effect on readers: what do we feel? How are we engaged?
- ☐ Analyse effect on readers: what do we learn?
- ☐ Use accurate spelling, punctuation and grammar.
- ☐ Write as many PEA-style paragraphs as you are able in the time available (c20-22 mins).

Appendix 1: How will my answer be assessed?

The exam board will assess your answer by checking to see how far you have met the Assessment Objective:

| AO2 | Understand and analyse how writers use linguistic and structural devices to achieve their effects. |

Top band answers are expected to show the following:

- Perceptive understanding and analysis of language and structure and how these are used by writers to achieve effects, including use of vocabulary, sentence structure and other language features.
- The selection of references is discriminating and clarifies the points being made.

This exam board language, however, can feel a bit technical or vague. After all, what do the exam board understand to be the difference between **understanding** and **analysis**? Who decides what the writers' **effects** are and whether they have been **achieved**? What makes a **reference selection** (quotation choice) **discriminating** rather than, as is expected of lower band answers, merely valid or appropriate?

In effect, it is your examiner who will judge how far you have **understood** and **analysed**, whether you have successfully identified **effects**, and whether your **reference selection** is sufficiently **discriminating**.

To help them, the examiner will be provided with a bullet point list of analyses students might make in answer to the exam question. This 'Indicative Content' is not exhaustive; examiners are encouraged to use their independent judgement about whether a point is valid even if it does not appear on the list provided by the exam board.

Ultimately, rather than answering questions about assessment objectives and mark schemes theoretically, the answers in this book aim to show in practical terms how it is possible to give your examiner what they are looking for, within the time constraints of the exam, whilst showing off the full range of your knowledge of how writers use the English language to communicate and create effects.

What makes these excellent exam answers?

There are many ways to organise information in an exam answer and you, or your teacher, may have different preferences about how to approach writing these answers. The model answers in this book reflect my judgement of what is the best approach based on my professional knowledge of what works for my students, my knowledge of what is readily readable by examiners and, perhaps most importantly, my own experience of writing these answers under timed conditions.

The ten answers here follow a consistent pattern:

- each answer is seven paragraphs long.
- each paragraph uses the PEA process to allow for embedding of carefully selected brief references (quotations) to back up my analysis.
- the PEA process is used with flexibility to avoid repetition and to allow for occasional instances where a point needs further evidence or further analysis to fully show my understanding of that particular moment in the text extract.
- each paragraph offers analysis of how the writers use language and/or structure to achieve their effects.
- each paragraph uses relevant subject terminology where appropriate.
- the first paragraph of each answer analyses an aspect of the early part of the text extract.
- subsequent paragraphs move the reader (examiner) through the rest of the extract.
- the final paragraph focuses on the ending of the text extract.

Thus, these answers manage to pack lots of detail into only around 500 words. The first drafts were written under the same conditions as the ones you will face (c20-22 minutes of writing time) and therefore reflect what is just about possible in such a short time. You may initially find it difficult to write so much detail in such a short space of time, but regular practice will definitely enable you to improve.

Best of luck in your exams!

Appendix 2: Acknowledgements

Quotations from works under copyright are fair dealing according to Section 30 of the Copyright, Designs and Patents Act 1988 (as amended) of the United Kingdom.

As such, the works quoted from are available to the public, the use of quotation is fair dealing with the work, the extent of the quotation is no more than is required by the specific purpose for which it is used, and the quotation is accompanied by a sufficient acknowledgement.

- Text from 'The Danger of a Single Story' by Chimamanda Ngozi Adichie, July 2009, https://www.ted.com/, copyright © Chimamanda Ngozi Adichie 2009.
- Text from *A Passage to Africa* by George Alagiah, Abacus, 2007, pp.87-90, copyright © George Alagiah 2001.
- Text from *The Explorer's Daughter* by Kari Herbert, Penguin, 2006, copyright © Kari Herbert 2004.
- An extract from 'Explorers, or Boys Messing About?' by Steven Morris, The Guardian, 28/01/2003, copyright © Guardian News & Media Ltd 2016.
- Text from *127 hours - Between a Rock and a Hard Place* by Aron Ralston, Simon & Schuster Ltd, 2010, pp.22-24, copyright © Aron Ralston 2004.
- Text from 'Young and Dyslexic? You've got it going on' by Benjamin Zephaniah, The Guardian, 02/10/2015, as adapted from *Creative, Successful, Dyslexic: 23 High Achievers Share Their Stories*, edited by Margaret Rooke, 2015.
- Text from *A Game of Polo with a Headless Goat* by Emma Levine, published by Andre Deutsch, copyright © Emma Levine 2000.
- Text from *Beyond the Sky and the Earth: A Journey into Bhutan* by Jamie Zeppa, Riverhead Books, 2000, copyright © Jamie Zeppa 1999.
- Text from *H is for Hawk* by Helen Macdonald, Jonathan Cape, 2014, copyright © Helen Macdonald 2014.
- Text from *Chinese Cinderella: The True Story of an Unwanted Daughter* by Adeline Yen Mah, Penguin, 1999, copyright © Adeline Yen Mah 1999.

Printed in Great Britain
by Amazon